Little Chicken Stories

Little Chicken Stories

A Primer for Keeping Chickens

A Chronicle of Backyard Escapades and Calamities

A Glimpse into the Kingdom of God

A Cookbook

* * *

Mary Rocap

ISBN-13: 978-0-557-74673-6
Design by April Leidig
Chicken photo credits: Tom Prince, Ann Rocap
Author photo credit: Laura Branan

With love to Tom

About the Author

Mary Rocap's life comes together on Saturday mornings when she heads out to the local farmers market to sell fresh baked bread, quilts and embroidered receiving blankets, eggs, CDs of original folk and gospel music, figs in the summer, and muscadines in the fall.

www.maryrocap.com

Author giving a reading at St. Matthew's. Note the chicken feather earrings.

Little Chicken Stories

Prologue: The Neighbor's Chickens

Tom and I had been married for 21 years before we found out that we shared a fascination for all things chicken. Somehow I had missed the warning signs: chicken calendars, chicken salt and pepper shakers, chicken refrigerator magnets. We were oblivious to the pull that chickens would have on our hearts.

Then, one Sunday morning in August 2005, out of the blue, we had eighteen chickens show up in our backyard. Astonishingly beautiful chickens: two roosters and sixteen hens of assorted plumage. Now, I had previously noticed neighbors with chickens in their front yard, so before going to church, I called them up and left a message wondering if they had noticed their chickens had gone missing, and did they think the birds would be smart enough to get back home. Well it turns out that I called the wrong neighbors — but I get ahead of the story. The neighbors I called did not return my phone call, and, actually, the chickens did leave at dusk. But the next day, and the next, and the next, they came back. It was like they came to work in the morning and went home at night.

We enjoyed watching them, we enjoyed talking about them and sharing funny things we had seen them do. We enjoyed their interactions with the environment, listening to their conversations, their calls, their warnings, their happy chuckles when we gave them sunflower seeds. We found ourselves counting them in the morning and counting them when we came home, worrying about what happened to the black one that hadn't showed up in a couple of days.

By October the flock was smaller and we started fretting about whether anyone was caring for them. What would happen when colder temperatures arrived? First we started putting out water, then some corn. By November we decided to build them a safe, warm coop.

Tom drew up a building plan, bought lumber, and the Saturday he hit the first nail into the first plank was the day we found out whose chickens they really were! I was walking in the woods where our property line meets our immediate neighbor's and he happened to be out there as well. At the end of the conversation, as I was turning away, he asks, "Say, are my chickens bothering you?" "Your chickens?! No, we love your chickens." It was with a heavy heart that I shared this knowledge of rightful ownership with Tom.

So, short of kidnapping the neighbor's flock, it was clear that if we wanted chickens to live in our coop, we would have to get some of our very own. We decided we would order some come spring. In the meanwhile, we enjoyed his flock, which continued to visit our yard and woods every day.

Our Own Chickens

We took the plunge. We ordered twenty-five brown egg layers and ten straight line (un-sexed) Buff Orpingtons from the hatchery Murray McMurray. This was a great bunch of chickens. The egg layers were an assortment of breeds and, as such, provided a lot of visual variety. We had Black Australorps, Dark Cornish, White Rocks, Rhode Island Reds, Silver Laced Wyandottes, a couple of feather-footed Light Brahmas, and a free exotic Silver Spangled Hamburg that we called Blue since he had blue shanks and feet.

We got them on Easter Monday, an ideal time for new life.

Tom brought home a huge cardboard box from work, which he

set up in our living room, along with a heat lamp and dispensers for water and food. The Postmaster called at 7:30 in the morning to say that our peeps had arrived, so we hurried off to bring them home. It is amazing to me that they made the trip in a perforated cardboard box from the hatchery in Iowa by U.S. Postal Service to North Carolina with no food or water shortly after hatching on Saturday. What an ordeal.

We picked up each chick, dipped its beak in sugar water, and set it in the waiting box. Immediately they understood that there is food and water here and start scratching and eating and drinking and running around and pooping. Without a Momma to show them what to do, they are quite self-sufficient.

It was when they were tired that they really missed a Momma's comforting presence. Instead of being able to go under her wing and breast for protection and warmth they would be in a standing position and then start to nod. With each succeeding breath they would nod deeper and lower, until at last they fell flat out on the floor surface, face down, neck stretched, wings extended. They looked dead. Alternatively, they would huddle together, climbing and clambering over one another to get into the most desired spot, usually in the corner or nearest the light. They peeped unless they were sleeping, calling for a Momma.

We have now had the experience of watching a Momma tend her brood, and the difference is remarkable. The chicks are quieter, calmer, never fall asleep exposed. It is much better for the chick to have someone who loves it nearby. And guess what — the chicks stay cuter longer. Our mail order chicks eat a grain with balanced nutrients that is designed for growth. Naturally raised chicks eat what their Momma gives them and grow more slowly.

I would be surprised if there is anyone out there who takes better care of little chicks than Tom. He creates a playground for them

Baby Blue in front

with rocks for them to climb on and small boxes for them to explore. He even "builds" an apartment complex by connecting two boxes with a hallway giving the chicks a choice of rooms to be in.

Well, we are empty nesters of a sort. Our elder daughter was in college and our younger daughter a very busy high school student, so maybe it's not too big a surprise that we invest some time and attention into these little bundles of life: these new responsibilities. We have to be home at night to close them in. We worry for their safety when we see dogs loose along the road or in the woods. Some have been given names. We think about their well being. It's not all about the eggs and meat. It's about being involved in another layer of creation and trying to be good stewards of some of Eden's descendants.

And, did I mention, they are highly entertaining?

The Garden of Eden

The man said, "The woman whom you gave to be with me, she gave me fruit from the tree, and I ate." — (Genesis 3:11)

If I believe anything in the Bible (and I do) then I believe in the truth of the opening chapters of Genesis: stories of creation and the Garden of Eden. Ancient stories, which describe the broken relationships between God and man, man and woman, man and creation, and the game of blame we've been playing ever since.

We had two dogs: Shadow and Zoë. Shadow was a black lab and a golden retriever mix. He had beautiful long black wavy hair. He was our first real pet and had lived with us all of our years in Cedar Grove. We got Zoë later to be a companion to Shadow. Zoë was a shepherd-huskie mix — white with blue eyes. So we had a black dog and a white dog, shadow and light, one male and one female. They were a good pair.

We kept our dogs penned. Orange County has leash laws even in the rural townships, which many people who live in out-lying sections ignore. Our neighbors, however, have sheep, and we didn't want to endanger them with our dogs running loose, especially since Zoë had a mind of her own and did not respond to command.

The free roaming chickens fascinated the dogs. Shadow and Zoë stalked them, quietly on the prowl from behind their prison bars. It seemed to me pretty obvious that a dog would be considered an ENEMY by a chicken, even a penned up dog, but the chickens must have gotten used to their presence, feeling safe with a fence between their living quarters.

What would possess a chicken to fly into the pen? Was it for the same reason a chicken crosses the road? (Answer: To show a possum it can be done.) Were they playing chicken? (Where does that expression come from?) Was the grass greener?

Whatever the motivation, this was the scene that greeted us one evening coming home from work: one dead chicken inside the pen, one unconcerned Zoë, and one nervous Shadow. Shadow, making a wide circle around the chicken carcass, came up to greet his returning masters, telling the whole story in his eyes and manner: "You wouldn't believe what happened today. I was minding my own business. That female, who you bought to be my companion, killed your bird. It was done before I knew what she was doing. I'm not responsible. It's all her fault. Don't be angry with me."

Zoë took the "Who me?" approach. "How dare you accuse me? The flying thing had a death wish."

Over time, Zoë killed three birds from inside the pen. Killing was something Zoë both liked and was good at, and maybe she dreamed what she would do if she ever got the chance to be a free agent. The months passed and she patiently waited until she got that chance.

One evening as I was slow to close the gate when bringing in dinner, she was quick to spot the opportunity. Out she went, not toward the chickens, but toward the road. She would not come when I called, but I knew she would be back and what she would be back for.

I stood guard, tried to shoo the chickens into their pen, but to no avail. With a predator instinct Zoë snuck in on a side flank; running with her head down low, she snapped up a buff hen.

That was it as far as I was concerned. We had recently lost Shadow to cancer and were fairly neutral in our regard for Zoë. So we took her back to the pound from whence she had come. Our daughters, both away for the summer, still have not forgiven us — perhaps with good reason. But our hearts had hardened against her, and it is doubtful we could have been persuaded to do otherwise.

So what about this little morality play acted out in the dog pen? What happened in the Garden of Eden didn't just happen way back when; it happens every day. Every morning brings both a new morning and a new fallen Eden as well. Our own original sin is committed over and over again. Even animals are not as immune from sin as we might like to imagine. Playing out the roles of Adam and Eve, God comes back to the garden and gets excuses. By now we ALL know the roles; we can play ALL the parts. We each participate in the cycle of birth and death, innocence and calculation, Eden and east of Eden, both man and beast.

Matters of Life & Death

THE SUMMER OF 2007 in the Piedmont of North Carolina was hot and dry. The average high was 96; the highest high was 105. August was the hottest and second driest month on record at the Raleigh Durham Airport (the official weather data collection spot in our area). Dogwoods were turning brown; poplars were losing yellowed leaves. The local growers of the Hillsborough Farmers' Market had given up irrigating, since no amount of watering seemed to quench the thirst of the soil, and their ponds were getting low. People asked politely about their neighbors' wells.

The end of summer was also when our friend Greg was trying to figure out why he had no energy and would shake with cold while running a fever. Turned out he had leukemia. He called me from the hospital just before a scheduled week of chemotherapy, saying he and his wife Carol were confident they could beat this. One week later, he was dead — a catastrophic reaction, from which he could not, did not, recover.

* * *

The heat stressed everybody, and it stressed our hens; they started laying fewer eggs as if to say, "Just be thankful we made it through another day." A day they had spent with their panting beaks open, seeking the shade and relative cool of the woods surrounding our home. Why one of the hens would decide to sit on a clutch during this hot spell is beyond me. But sit she did, in the coop where temperatures surely were 10 degrees above the actual. She had laid claim to eight eggs.

After three weeks of her sitting, looking mean, and poofing out when approached, there was movement and a little head shyly peeking out from her breast where she sat on her nest. By the end of the day there were three little fluff balls, a buff and two with shades of gray coloration. The next day she left her nest, abandoning the five remaining eggs, and took her little brood down the plank to the fenced area under the coop. We rejoiced at her accomplishment in the face of such adverse conditions.

That evening we caused a panic as Tom decided it was time to confine an increasingly pesky rooster. There was chaos and pandemonium. The little chicks fled through the fence, but Momma was trapped. Tom's and my attention were completely focused on the rooster, and so didn't appreciate the desperate situation we had created for Momma. She eventually got herself over the 6-foot high fence and shot like a bat from hell through the woods in hot pursuit of her babes.

At that point the situation we had created sunk in, and we went into search and rescue mode. We listened for peeps, couldn't hear any. We walked slowly through the woods looking for movement, didn't see any. It was an hour 'til dusk and time was short.

Alas, we did not find them. We delayed closing up the birds 'til well after dark, hoping they would return. We felt like idiots.

This was within days of receiving word of Greg's death. At our very late dinner, Tom prayed "Thy will be done." To which I involuntarily moaned, "No." I wasn't ready for another dose of God's will.

The next morning I went out looking for Momma and her chicks. I went to the hen house and was surprised to find one of the five remaining eggs had a crack in it. I picked it up, and it peeped! Completely taken aback, I squeezed it slightly, and it peeped again. Who knew a chick peeped before hatching? Who knew that eggs cool to the touch, abandoned a whole day would be viable?

I picked up all five eggs and hurried inside, making a little nest in a basket and setting it under the heat lamp that was warming our ten-day old mail-order chicks housed in a big box in our living room. I called work and said I would be late, called my Mom and Dad to see if they wanted to come over and watch with me, and called Tom with the good news.

In fact, while the sound of the peep was good news, I learned it takes some time and effort for a chick to hatch. The egg shudders and shakes. Eventually, more of the shell opened, and we could see a little beak with its egg tooth and some of the body. The body pulsed like a little heart, straining against the constraints of the shell. Surprisingly, the membrane seemed to pose the most difficulty, tearing separately from the breaking of the shell. I called my neighbor Joy, who has a lot more experience in these matters, and she counseled against helping the chick out of the shell (which I was inclined to do). She said it is the effort of the chick against the shell that makes the chick ready to stand after hatching.

Realizing this is a solitary task for the chick I reluctantly left for work. Mom said she would check in on the progress. At 12:30 she reported that we had the cutest little fluffy buff chick.

What good and amazing news!

When I got home late afternoon, wonder-of-wonders, Momma was back with her three little ones. We introduced her new one to her, and she accepted it with solemnity.

I know that human life, the life of my friend Greg, is not comparable to the lives of my little birds. He was a close friend, my best song critic, a wise and compassionate person. I miss him. Yet I know that God loves all of his creation — all creatures great and small. It is written that God knows when every sparrow falls ("Yet not one of them is forgotten in God's sight." Luke 12:6) and those words resonate in me. I love the song "His Eye is on the Sparrow," with its corollary line: "and I know he cares for me," made famous by Ethel Waters. And in truth, the miraculous life of these little birds has been some comfort.

Life is a mystery. In the end, we don't know what death is or what purpose it serves. It pleases me that Momma and her chicks' lives were spared; it hurts that Greg's life was taken, and that hurt will stay hurt a long time. "The Lord giveth, the Lord taketh away. Blessed be the name of the Lord." (Job 1:21) I have to try to offer both the rejoicing and the mourning to God and claim, by faith, that death is not the end, but a new beginning. Life will have the last word, not death.

And so, journey on Greg.

Seeking a New Community

FOR SOME REASON, our Rhode Island Reds were the favorite targets for the procreative attentions of our roosters. Maybe they are the slowest runners or the meekest or the most attractive. I don't know. I just know that the roosters really were hard on them. You know it's bad when a hen's back has been denuded of feathers and a patch of skin shows through. I'm not proud that our management of the rooster population led to this, but we have had a learning curve to master, and we have a better rooster to hen ratio now.

We had three reds, all with skin showing, but one was in worse shape than the others. She seemed depressed about her situation and tried to avoid the roosters at all cost even withdrawing from the comfort of flock membership. She would be the last to leave the coop in the morning and spent her days alone. She maintained a low profile by hiding under a parked car, in the unused dog pen, or around the shed. At night she would make a dash to the coop, trying to sneak around the posted sentry cocks.

One day, as I was visiting my folks, who live next door to us, the timid red hen approached the sheep which are boarded on their property. She waddle-bounced over to the fence, and the sheep came over to greet her. As she was on the ground, one of the sheep lowered his face until it met hers. She then hopped up on the fence so that she was on his eye-level. They interacted about ten minutes, and we commented that it looked like she was seeking admittance into his community. I clearly expected her to hop onto the sheep's back and ride off into the sunset.

She didn't.

Instead she came over to our table and hopped onto the bench as we sat on it. This was highly unusual behavior. She was so intentional. If she could not have the sheep's protection, then she would seek ours. At that point we noticed that she was injured. So I picked her up and took her home.

Tom washed her wound, and then we decided to isolate her from the rest of the flock a couple of days so that she could heal. This we did.

The day of her release, I noticed she had not returned to the coop with the others in the evening. Knowing her hiding spots I went looking for her. Once found, I picked her up and took her to the coop myself. This pattern continued. She would stay hidden even though two roosters would be sent out to look for her at dusk. They would sally forth on their reconnaissance mission, call and listen, and then return to the coop unsuccessful. Then I would walk out, and when she heard my footsteps, she would come out from her hiding place, allow me to pick her up and take her to bed with the others. After a couple of weeks, she got up her nerve and returned to the coop on her own.

One night, we awoke to a distress cry from the coop, and I realized I had forgotten to close up the birds. We went out quickly, but the damage had already been done.

Interestingly enough, #1 and #3 rooster were down below out of the coop, number #2 remained inside. (Perhaps a good battle plan.) And we were shocked to see that a raccoon was still on the premises, climbing the fence in the back, making his escape. We spent about one-half hour in the middle of the night trying to round up the birds to go back inside.

Initially, we thought we had lost some, since the following morning the count was down. But it turned out that a few had fled into the woods only to return the following night. The picked-on red was the only one that stayed missing. There is something to jungle logic that weakest ones are the ones taken.

I feel bad that I let the chickens down in my care. They are completely defenseless at night — picked-on chickens as well as chickens that do the picking-on. And I feel bad that the one that needed my care the most suffered the most for its lack.

It's a mean, hard world out there being subject of both the pecking order and food chain. Our clumsy interventions do not always pay off and perhaps are misguided to boot.

Consulting with the sheep.

Consulting with the humans.

Murder in the Ranks

There are distinct job descriptions and behaviors for the alpha rooster and roosters #2 and below. For example, non-dominant roosters:

* check the coop before hens enter at night, round up the stragglers, and are the last in at night
* are denied shelter during a rain storm
* stay close to the hens when they are laying
* arbitrate hen fights
* hit on hens if the alpha rooster is not around
* challenge the alpha rooster at any opportunity they feel up to it

The dominant rooster:

* notifies everyone when he finds food and it is especially good
* has unchallenged access to the hens
* defends his alpha status at all times
* is the primary cockadoodledooer
* responds to distress calls
* is the main defender of the flock

We knew we had too many roosters. The hens knew it too. But killing roosters has not been an easy task. It took us a good old time to get the numbers down from six to two in our mature flock. We were left with a Buff Orpington who was the alpha and Blue, the Silver Spangled Hamburg, who we kept primarily for his looks.

It may have been that #1 got sick because his behavior started to alter in a strange way. He became more of a loner. Maybe he was tired out and needed a break. Roosters have a shorter life span than hens. Blue had been so far down the rooster dominance scale he never even seemed like a contender, but when we killed all the others he rose to the occasion. He looked good, strong, and was full of himself. He started challenging the Buff all the time.

One morning Blue would not let the Buff alone. He was relentless and spirited. The Buff was running from him rather than defending himself. Both Tom and I noticed it and spoke about it before going off to work.

When I came home, I found the Buff dead in the coop.

I think Blue done him in. Since then, he's the alpha and doesn't look as good. He's lost his flouncy tail feathers and his white hackles are looking yellow-tinged. The generation behind him has a rooster that's looking pretty sharp.

It's hard work being alpha. You've got to prove yourself all the time both with the ladies and the men. Watch out Blue, you've got some competition. The competition is serious and can be deadly.

Symphony in the Key of G

I AM NOT A PHYSICIST but as a musician I appreciate the concept of string theory — all of creation, every elementary particle, is made up of strings, which vibrate. Vibration produces tone. We are quite literally music to God's ears.

All religions use music to express themselves spiritually. I think it is safe to say that humans have discovered that God loves music. In addition to Psalms, a whole book of songs, there are many references to music in our scripture. John, the revelator, richly describes a vision that was "like the sound of harpists playing on their harps, and [singing] a new song before the throne." And again, "I looked, and I heard the voice of many angels surrounding the throne . . . they numbered myriads of myriads, and thousands of thousands, singing with full voice. Then I heard every creature in heaven and on earth and under the earth and in the sea, and all that is in them, singing." (from Revelations 5)

Our simply being alive is pleasing to God. We are both melody and harmony. As children of God, we love music too. In fact, we seem to have an insatiable need for it. I never tire of listening to music, even to pieces I have heard time and time again. It seems that familiarity heightens enjoyment.

The animal kingdom also has a musical bent. I do not believe the wood thrush sings just to find a mate. The unearthly beauty of his song sounds like worship to me. Sometimes when I go to close up the chickens at nightfall, I hear one making hushed, sweetly pitched, humming sounds. To me it is a lullaby, a benediction upon the day, a compline prayer.

I have noticed that the sounds of nature are very integrated and tuneful. The rise and fall of the ocean waves coming to shore is not out of sync with the call of the sea bird, the sound of my footsteps, or the laughter of my children at play. They go together in a mysterious way; they are one piece: a symphony, a symphony in the Key of God.

Now, I happen to think that Richard Strauss wrote some of the most beautiful music ever composed. When I want to feel transported I listen to the final trio in his opera, *Der Rosenkavalier.* The tension and release of that score never fails to move me. Whenever I have a lengthy project around the house and am alone, that opera is my first choice of music to accompany the task.

I did have a room-painting project recently and so I put on the opera. While I was painting, I was also in earshot of my chickens, and the roosters from time to time, were crowing. Do you know that I had to pause and consider this: was that part of the opera, or was that a rooster? There was something about the interval of the notes hit in the cockledoodledoo that were surprisingly similar to the intervals in the themes of Strauss. Now, while this may make non-opera fans conclude that I am saying Strauss sounded like screeching birds, I assure you, quite the opposite. I am now, more than ever, of the mind that Strauss' writing is akin to worship. There is no disharmony between his work and that of the natural world, or in this case, the chicken world.

All our strings are vibrating, producing an all powerful "Amen" to the Creator and Sustainer of the universe. Children and chickens of God: Life itself is a song, raise your voice and sing.

Of Peeps and Bunnies

EASTER IS A JOYFUL TIME. Spring is upon us. The bees are buzzing. It feels good to be alive. To celebrate the season and the day we buy pink and yellow marshmallow peeps with a shelf life of centuries. We consume enormous, hollow, milk chocolate rabbits with features of colored icing. And, we boil eggs, dip them in colored vinegar solution, take them outside, and hide them for our children to "discover."

My daily egg hunting is a mini Easter Egg Hunt. I take my woven egg basket out into the yard and hen house just like a child, and am always grateful for what I find, thanking whatever hen is within earshot as I go. The eggs are beautiful to me: sometimes warm, always satisfying to hold in my hand. There is a quality of perfection about them, which may explain why the ancient Persians believed earth hatched from a giant egg.

Eggs and bunnies have long been symbols of spring. The practice of dying eggs in spring colors began in Egypt and Persia. They were given away as gifts. Christians in Mesopotamia assimilated this custom as part of their Easter celebrations. Germany was responsible for the tradition of Easter bunnies bringing Easter eggs.

According to legend, a poor woman dyed eggs during a time of famine and hid them for her children to find on Easter morning. When the children discovered the eggs, a big rabbit leapt away, leading to the tale of the rabbit bringing eggs to children that has spread far and wide.

One year, on an Easter morning, Tom, who had been outside, came in saying, "Come quickly! Come see what I've found." We went, following him out to the garden, which was blooming in a knee-high cover crop of crimson clover. He had inadvertently disturbed a nest of bunnies. There they were in a little burrow — about six of them — tiny, tiny, furry bunnies. These Real Easter Bunnies became a treasured memory. They did not bring us colored eggs, but they were in their very being, a symbol of new life.

Another Easter memory I have is when the girls were out egg hunting in the yard and Christy mistook a real black snake for a rubber black snake that she knew her Daddy Tom owned. She picked it up without fear, instantly releasing it when she realized her mistake. Not everything out in the world is welcoming on an Easter morning!

For all their popularity, Easter eggs, candy peeps, and chocolate bunnies don't tell the story of Easter. Although, at our church, St. Matthew's Episcopal, we have a tradition that makes use of these symbols and gets closer to the truth. On Easter morning, after the Great Vigil, after the cross has been decorated with spring flowers, the young children, dressed in their finery, are released for the Annual Easter Egg Hunt. Brightly colored plastic eggs filled with treats have been hidden in the churchyard — the graveyard — a symbol whose meaning may be lost on the children running from grave to grave looking for their eggs.

Mary may have run from tomb to tomb looking for her Jesus. "What have you done with his body?" she asks the gardener. "Mary" he says to her, and she recognizes her Lord. Life trumps death. Life exploded from the grave. The angels ask her companions, "Why do you look for the living among the dead? Tell the others that he is going ahead of you to Galilee." Jesus was on the move. Now, as then, he goes ahead showing us the way. And like Peter, John, and the other disciples who joined him in Galilee, so too do we follow his footsteps.

Along the way, our journey is full of signs and wonders. Is not the hatching of a chick a thing of wonder? If we look closely, we will find myriad symbols of broken eggs, which newly hatched peeps have abandoned. Life cannot be contained. It's exploding all over.

Alleluia. Christ is risen.
Christ is risen indeed. Alleluia.

This is the Easter acclamation. Easter is a time to celebrate new life — a life that triumphs over death. Hmm, I feel like dying some of my eggs bright spring colors!

Egg Gathering

We moved to Cedar Grove in 1997. Cedar Grove is outside of Hillsborough, which is outside of Chapel Hill and Durham, which means it's country for now but getting less so with each passing year.

We have seventeen acres — mostly wooded, with two streams and so we call the place GatherCreek. We are not farmers, we have too many day jobs for that, but Tom has planted muscadine and scuppernong grapes, pecans, apples, and figs. He usually starts a garden with high hopes but spring or summer invariably does something unhelpful and squashes the plan.

I am a craftsperson in addition to church secretary, bookkeeper, and singer-songwriter/musician. I make quilts and embroidered baby blankets and other hand crafted and sewn articles. I sell them at the local farmers market on Saturday mornings. I also sell eggs.

Since our hens are pastured and roam freely, they do not necessarily lay their eggs where I think they should lay them — in the coop's conveniently placed laying shelves. I haven't figured out a good reward structure for hens. If you take away the egg they just laid isn't that negative reinforcement? Occasionally we'll find an egg on the ground. Hens generally, though, are creatures of habit and will lay their eggs in the same place every day (or every day they lay). Sometimes a hen will get a notion to try a new spot and we won't know for a while where it is. My folks' property next door has many appealing sites.

The qualities of a good laying spot are that it is quiet, protected, and smallish. Corners are especially favored. Older hens model the behavior for the younger ones. I have started leaving plastic Easter eggs in the coop, hoping the hens are colorblind and won't notice or be disturbed by a completely artificial bright blue or orange egg. I have these times when I feel that, despite our steady affection and care, they're holding out on us. When we have introduced a new generation to the flock, production has decreased. It's some kind of revenge —"So I'm not good enough for you; well, I won't give you my eggs." Things that we've discovered to affect egg production are: a change in routine, summer's heat, winter's cold, aging hens, a moult, a broody cycle. Illness also can be a factor.

The eggshell is the last part of the egg making process. Sometimes an egg is laid that has the membrane but not the shell. That is very odd looking. It has an egg shape but is soft and pliable. Eggs do not always have the perfect shape that you expect if you have only had store-bought eggs. Sometimes they are rough, or spotted, or misshapen, or have extra calcium deposits that look like warts. They come in different colors. Even brown eggs are varied in hue.

Eggs should be gathered every day and refrigerated immediately and constantly. Washing them with soap and water is discouraged; wipe them off with a damp towel if they are dirty. When an egg is just laid it is wet. This wet substance, called bloom, dries into a protective coating for the shell. It is better that this remains on the egg than be washed off. Eggshells are porous allowing for the exchange of gases for a maturing chick. Storing eggs small end down in the egg carton rather than an open container in the refrigerator will reduce evaporation. Eggs will keep a long time. Their flavor and texture will deteriorate over time but I have yet to eat an egg of ours that seems stale.

My eggs are labeled ungraded, which means they are not sized by weight. Most of the vendors who sell eggs sell them as ungraded. Fresh eggs are a draw for any farmers market. I'm always surprised at how quickly someone will pay premium prices for eggs that will be gone in a week and then turn around and say that my potholders are too expensive and yet they will last years as an adornment or tool in their kitchen. I guess Mary, the crafter, may be a little jealous of Mary, the egg-gatherer!

Mirror Mirror on the Wall

MIRRORS ARE PART OF the human world — not so much a part of the animal kingdom. Any smooth surface that reflects light, rather than absorbs its rays, is a mirror. The higher the polish, the greater the reflection. I know the taste of the apple was the ruin of first Eve and then Adam, but, while the mirror is not mentioned in the ancient text, I'll bet it was not far behind, running a close second to the fruit.

We want to see ourselves; we are fascinated with our own image. Mythology tells us that the downfall of Lucifer was pride. Since the Latin root of his name means "light bringing," and mirrors are by definition reflectors of light, I see a relationship of idea or meaning. What do we see when we look into a mirror? What do we look for? Do we see the reflection of one created in the image of God or do we seek to be gods ourselves?

Whatever the basis, mirrors are everywhere. We look at ourselves as soon as we wake up and just before going to bed when we brush our teeth or brush our hair. Whole buildings are erected with mirror exteriors; we send mirrors into space. I'm not saying mirrors are not useful. For example, mirrors in the car allow me to see where I am in relation to those behind or on either side. I'm just saying they are everywhere. If you want to look at yourself, you can, within seconds of the desire.

To illustrate this point, I was sitting with my band mates before a gig in the green room at The Carrboro ArtsCenter and I had mirrors on my mind, since I had in the morning just started working on this very story. Two people who worked for the club came in with a mirror (!), asked whether we would mind if they installed it, and then, receiving permission, proceeded to lay it between some open slats of the ceiling. It was not a very highly polished surface and so not a very effective looking glass. Nor did it have a sturdy back and once hung took on a convex shape. Looking up at our reflections we saw blurry, short, and round rock 'n rollers looking back.

Our oldest daughter, in her preparations for college, needed a full-length mirror for her room. Wanting to personalize it, she went into my button collection and decorated the frame with an assortment of colored buttons. Back and forth we took this to college at the beginning and end of each school year.

The chickens seem to hang out close to home when we are

around so they were all out in the yard as we were loading up the jeep. I slung the mirror against my hip and walked out to the car.

Well, the chickens had never seen their world, themselves reflected back to them, and they were not even curious; they were frightened. Suddenly, double the number of chickens seemed present, the sky was fractured and moving, and trees, out of proportion, appeared out of nowhere. A cry of alarm went up and they scattered into the woods for protection.

I came away from this episode with both a chuckle over the silliness of our birds to be scared by their reflections and a greater appreciation of how our actions affect them. The next time I carried the mirror, I was more circumspect and the chickens had a calmer afternoon.

Hawk 27 : Humans 0

I'VE GOT TO RAISE MY HAT to the prowess of the hawk as a bird of prey. We have a red-tailed hawk eating all his meals at our hen house, and we have been powerless to stop him. He goes after our teenagers — our three-month-olds. It is very depressing to come home to fewer and fewer birds. The pathetic attempts we make to discourage him: stringing up pie pans, making a scarecrow don't do any good.

Short of totally fencing in the top of the pen and keeping the birds enclosed at all times, there doesn't seem to be a good reasonably priced alternative. Sure they would be alive but it's not the life we want our birds to live. Not much different from the VOLUME chicken operation by a neighbor who keeps 13,000 birds in each of two chicken houses. Have you ever seen 13,000 chickens in a confined space? He collects 10,000 eggs every day. I think I am doing well when I collect nine. No, we don't want our birds enclosed.

We hope that since the hawk has not gone after the older birds once he has taken the easy prey he will move on. The hawk does not even take his kill off with him. He eats a little, enough to satiate him, and then leaves the rest. This is so wasteful! If he would just eat the whole thing, or take it home to finish later, he would not be hungry so soon nor return as quickly for another meal. It would give my birds some more time to get bigger.

I have seen Blue challenge the hawk: standing in a clearing, #2 on the side line ready to assist if needed, hens in the woods, Blue calling and calling for the hawk to come and fight, to pick on someone his own size. My Mom has seen Blue charge the hawk. Good job Blue.

Hawks are protected — you can't kill one intentionally. And in truth, they have a part to play in the balance of nature. They are fabulous hunters with eyesight eight times more acute than our own. We have plenty of other animal life I wouldn't mind losing to the hawk, such as squirrels, rabbits, or voles.

Sometimes they are referred to as chicken hawks and I can see why. On the ground, I have mistaken the hawk for a chicken, but then he opens up these massive wings, and off he goes. Chickens don't fly like that.

Our teenage birds may have been intellectually challenged. They traveled in mass, were homebodies; they chose to stay inside the coop or pen rather than explore the woods, where they would have been safer. One day I came home and saw the hawk take off from inside the pen. He failed to get a bird on that attempt. It was only later I noticed that, in their desperation to get away, the first bird to get to the corner actually was suffocated or crushed by the ones rushing in afterwards.

The hawk has also, I regret to report, taken three of Momma's four chicks. I will say this on her behalf: she did a better job at keeping her babies alive than we did. She lost 75% of her brood; we lost 92%.

I do not intend to update this story with any future occurrence. As far as I am concerned, Momma's last baby lived, and our two remaining teenagers lived as well, even if it is only in this story and only on this page.

Go live somewhere else hawk. I happen to know a place where thousands of chickens live — not that far away.

A Confused Broody Hen

ONE HEN FROM OUR initial flock, a Dark Cornish, decided she was momma material shortly after we introduced our second flock to the year-old "only children." It was almost like seeing a bunch of little chicks must have turned a light on for her with the notion "Hey, I think I know how that happens. I think I have a part to play and, I think I know what it is."

Being a sitting hen does not come as naturally as you might suppose. This trait has been mostly bred out of her. We prize the hen for her eggs and meat, not her mothering skills. But the Dark Cornish is supposed to be a good sitter and mother. We were very excited about her sitting on a clutch but realized she, unfortunately, didn't exactly know what she was doing, even though she acted the part quite well.

It takes about three weeks of sitting to hatch a chick. This task completely changes the activity and behavior of the hen. She becomes protective of her nest. She rarely leaves it, rushing out only for quick meals and water breaks. She rotates the eggs, keeping their temperature even and not allowing the eggs to stay just in one position. If the eggs stay in one position they will not mature correctly. The yolk is attached at either end of the shell by strands of filament, which suspend the yolk in the center of the egg. If the eggs are not rotated, the yolk will adhere to a side instead of floating in the center and the new life is doomed. It takes great dedication and focus for the momma to hatch her chicks.

We were pretty sure the eggs she was sitting on were fertile. At the time we had three highly active roosters. She set up shop on the far side of the top right hand side of the coop. She was sitting on six eggs.

One day I arrived home and found she was sitting on the lower far side of the coop. Upstairs were two lonely eggs. What happened to the other four? Why was she downstairs?

I brought the two eggs down and set them close to her saying, "Honey, you've lost your eggs." She looked at them and then with her beak gently brought them both to and under her, one at a time.

Over the course of the next week, I found her in various locations in the coop, sometimes sitting on eggs, sometimes not. She continued to maintain her protective behavior and focused glare. All total she spent about five weeks in her broody cycle, finally abandoning five unhatched eggs. When she hadn't returned to her nest after three days, I broke the eggs, curious about their stage of development. Only one showed signs of early chickenhood.

I'm not really sure what happened. Had a snake frightened her off and eaten her eggs? Did she herself or another hen eat them? Had she seen newly laid eggs and become confused or decided to start the process over? Anyway, it didn't work out that time but she must have learned something since later that summer she went broody again, and this time was successful.

Don't Count Your Chickens . . .

When we had our first batch of chickens, they were easy to count: three Rhode Island Reds, ten Buffs, one white rooster, you get the idea — smaller numbers within the flock added up to 36. I could isolate the parts and come up with an accurate total. Since then there have been additions to the flock and attrition from the flock, making the total count a number in flux.

Our current flock is mostly one kind, and I find it impossible to count them when they are out and about. The flock is a moving target — on the go constantly. I get mixed up wondering if I counted that one already and so have to start over repeatedly. I'm not entirely sure how many I should have and end up befuddled with the thought, "Well, it looks like a fair number, so I guess they're all here."

The only time I can count with assurance is when I count at night. Then they are all perched on their roosts in the coop and I can take the flashlight in and count their stationary heads.

They say that no two snowflakes are alike. I have a hard time truly believing this except that I know God is highly creative and is not one to run out of ideas or get into a rut. If there are differences between snowflakes, surely there must be differences between chickens. But can I tell the difference between two of the same breed? Mostly, no! Some have behavioral traits that separate one from another. Others, through wear and tear, end up with different physical features. But it is only the noticeably different that ends up with a name.

A crowd of people or a flock of birds is an impersonal group until you recognize an individual member. Identifying a face, knowing a name is the beginning of relationship, of connection. When a child is born, the first thing I want to know is what the newborn is to be called. Our name is one of the first gifts we receive and perhaps the most lasting.

Maybe this is why Adam was tasked with naming the creatures in God's world. Naming led to relationship, relationship to care and responsibility.

The naming of creatures is common to all cultures, whereas things like numbering or describing shades of color are not. I know I listen way too much to National Public Radio, but I've learned some interesting things along the way. One report described a culture with a very minimal numbering system: basically it was one vs. many / enough vs. more than enough. Another culture described colors only in warm (red) tones or cool (blue) tones. Hence the designated color for sky and tree was the same word.

We've come a long way from Adam in the naming department. Over time we have become increasingly specific. Scientifically, chickens belong to the animal kingdom, the chordata phylum, the vertebrata subphylum, the aves class, the Galliformes order, the Phasiansidae family, the Gallus genus, the G. domesticus species, and finally a breed variety. The chicken nickname, scientifically speaking, is Gallus domesticus. The semi-personal names we have given our chickens have been based on the roles they play (Momma) or by their relative age in relation to the flock in general (our teenagers). Only a few have rated a bonafide personal name (Blue, Goldie, Bucky). They were named because they stood out — and because they had names we took notice of them even more, and they became the ones we loved the most. Naming was the start of relationship.

God is the only one big enough to know all his creatures. He recognizes all faces in the crowd, can call by name all the sheep in his pasture. His capacity to know and love is boundless. With time and study, I probably could recognize all my chickens within the flock at which point I could account for them by name, rather than by number, and know if one was missing.

Until then, when asked, "How many chickens do you have?" and, knowing I am a less than accurate counter, I simply answer "Well, more than enough."

Bucky and Goldie's Brood

GOLDIE AND BUCKY WERE the last survivors of the neighbor's chickens. They were a pair of Brown Leghorns. Bucky's coloration was glorious: fine deep turquoise tail feathers, burnt orange, rust, and iridescent black in his wings and body. I was so taken with his plumage that I created an entire full-sized quilt using the palette of his feathers.

They eventually stopped going home at dusk after their workday and started roosting in our pines. They changed their roost from time to time — perhaps defensively. They would spend the day within our flock and then at dusk turn away and head into the woods. Once under the canopy, they would look up, stretch their necks, and with a burst of wing power ascend into the heights. Coming down at dawn would be proceeded with a loud "Geronimo" or "Here I come ready or not" yell. When Goldie got broody her nest site was in the coop, so Bucky went to bed alone.

We were so excited. She sat on six eggs and successfully hatched them all: adorable fluffy chicks, of different hue. While the clutch was not all her eggs, just one day's laying that she decided to claim as hers, the daddy was Bucky. I was delighted that we might have another Bucky in our future.

While the new brood stayed in the coop, they were protected, but once Goldie brought them down the plank into the penned area, they were not safe. Raccoons, possum, snakes, owls, or hawks could all get in quite easily. Going up the plank was hard for the little ones and Goldie would not tolerate our help in the process.

So we tried to fortify an area for them under the coop. We brought in an old doghouse, and Goldie liked that. She shepherded her brood inside there for the night. Once in, we barricaded the door with a metal sheet and then rested a cement block against it. This was successful for a number of nights.

Then one morning came and we found the cement block dislodged, the metal sheet on the ground, Goldie outside the doghouse, and all six chicks gone.

For three days Goldie stayed in the yard calling for her babes. It was a mournful and desperately sad sight. She was bereft and keenly felt the loss; I cried over the loss as well.

After those three days she returned to roosting in the pines with Bucky, living alongside of but not a part of the flock. Eventually, Bucky left our property to seek his fortune with the neighbors across the road. Goldie stayed behind. After several months we stopped seeing her as well. Maybe she followed him or was taken by a predator — we just don't know.

We ordered some baby Brown Leghorns to take their place and now call all the girls Goldie, but we haven't given the name Bucky to any of the guys. Not a one is as fine a looker as he.

Chickens, chickens everywhere

THE GREAT-GREAT-GREAT-grandparents of chickens are the jungle fowl of Southeast Asia. As long as 5,000 years ago humans discovered there was value in taming and raising these birds for eggs and meat. From this common ancestor there are now more than 50 standard breeds and from these 50 breeds come more than 180 varieties or recognized hybrids, not to mention unrecognized outcomes of disorganized natural selection. As people of the world came into contact with each other through trade or conquest so did chickens expand into different climes and cultures.

We didn't know about the famous Key West chickens when we went there to celebrate our 25th wedding anniversary. We didn't even know Key West had chickens. But the Spanish, Bahamians, and Cubans who settled Key West in the 1800s brought them along. The Spanish brought Mediterranean breeds such as the Leghorn and Minorca. The Cubans brought Bantams raised for cockfighting. Somewhere along the way chickens were abandoned by their owners or escaped from captivity and went native. From jungle fowl ancestry to birds living in a resort town, this small island today is inhabited by some 2,000 what the locals call "gypsy" chickens.

Key West is a great place for walking and after a sunset dinner on the dock we took a stroll. We were walking down Duvall Street when something made me turn around. There strutting across the street in blackened silhouette was the shape of a rooster. What, hey. Tell me I didn't just see what I think I saw. I must be missing my chickens so much I am imagining they are here with me.

We turned around and tried to find the source of this vision but couldn't find him. We continued on our way Tom questioning my sanity.

The following morning on a stroll in search of coffee and breakfast we both heard a rooster crow, an unmistakable rooster crow, shortly followed the sight of a small flock of chickens looking a lot like our old pals Bucky and Goldie. What was unusual about this flock was that it was equally made up of male and female birds.

I had never seen a naturalized flock of chickens before. I have seen either flocks made of all hens raised for their eggs or ones of all cockerels raised for meat but never a flock of made up of equal parts.

As the little flock of eight scratched for food the roosters stood at the compass points with the hens on the inside of the circle. The roosters weren't fighting or chasing each other off. It looked like a calm, well adjusted, friendly family of birds engaged in the business of finding something to eat.

When we questioned the concierge of the hotel about what we had seen we learned that the community of Key West is not so fond of their gypsy chicken population. They are seen as noisy nuisances and the town has tried various schemes to reduce their population including hiring a chicken catcher for a short time in 2003. They gave up that approach because of negative publicity and since then they have had an uneasy truce since the tourists find the presence of chickens appealing.

In every gift shop chicken kitsch is bountiful. There are chicken postcards, bookends, salt and peppershakers, and t-shirts. I admit I succumbed and bought a set of rooster and hen figurines, which now sit atop a table in the living room. They serve as a reminder of our of anniversary trip to Key West, dinners on the dock at sunset, music on the street, key lime pies, crystal blue water, and the gypsy birds we found there.

Be Here Now

I HAVE THIS FAVORITE JOKE: But on the other hand . . . you have five fingers.

What this has to do about *Be Here Now* I'm not totally sure. It is possible it will become clearer to me as I write.

I have a confession to make. Collecting eggs is somewhat terrifying to me when the hen is sitting on the nest while I am trying to take her progeny. Let's just say hens don't always take this lightly. No matter what the temperature now I prepare myself for battle.

I put on crummy shoes that won't mind the muck of the pen and a long sleeved denim work shirt to protect my hands, wrists, and lower arms. I go in with a song on my lips, I greet the hens and tell them what I am up to, I move slowly but deliberately so as to accomplish my task but not scare them, and above all I try not to be intimidated by them. But know that I will not go in the hen house if the rooster is in there even though he has never showed any mean-spiritedness to me. I have my limits.

The hens do not all react the same to collecting eggs. And not all the hens will linger with the eggs they lay. Most of them have better things to do. But a hen may linger if she is tired or broody or lazy. Through the experience of collecting eggs I have noticed a difference amongst the breeds in so far as defending the nest goes. Collecting from White Rocks is a piece of cake. They act unconcerned and will grant me permission by standing up thus easing my access to their eggs. A Buff Orpington makes a whinny horse-like sound, ruffles up her feathers but it's all show — bark but no bite. Sometimes one will mistake my hand for an egg and try to corral me using her wings and thighs to position me under her broody body. I kinda like that.

It is the Dark Cornish that I truly dread. They will hiss and peck with a wide open beak trying to get as much of my flesh as possible. Some will even try to protect the adjoining nest box, which as far as I am concerned should be no business of hers. A chicken can be fierce in defense of her eggs. I can only pick up two eggs at a time and a hen can be sitting on up to maybe eight eggs so I have to go in repeatedly to get all the eggs she may have. This will allow the hen time to better position herself and plan her next attack.

The thing is sometimes in her drive to protect the eggs a hen will inadvertently peck at the egg instead of my hand. Usually no matter, the eggshell is hard enough to sustain a blow. But I have had an egg crack and break as a result of a particularly effective peck. When this has happened, immediately the hen will discard the protection behavior and launch into FOOD procurement behavior and start to eat the contents of the egg.

There is no element of surprise, alarm, or loss. Plan A is traded in for Plan B. Food has just appeared at my doorstep. I will eat. There is literally no transition time. It is instantaneous.

Now, it is not as though chickens never show any sense of loss-remember how Momma cried for the loss of her chicks. But death and life are accepted readily. They simply move on.

When I was in college in the early 70s the "be here now" slogan was prevalent. And, in truth, living in the present is commendable. Solomon, after all, councils us to eat, drink, and be merry, for tomorrow we die. We are not to wallow in the past nor work just for the future. In a sense that hen was living out these words from Ecclesiastes: "For everything there is a season, and a time for every matter under heaven: a time to be born, and a time to die; a time to plant, and a time to pluck up what is planted; a time to kill, and a time to heal." (Ecclesiastes 3:1-3a)

And yet, and yet, her actions are too blunt for me. I don't want to forget the past so quickly. I want to be alive to the present while remembering what has gone before and hoping for what is to come. Sometimes there are lessons I learn from my birds, but I think I'm going to pass on this one.

But on the other hand . . . you have five fingers.

I can't think of a way to tie in my joke after all. Maybe it's just there to amuse you as it does me.

Birds of a Feather . . .
It's true they stick together.

EVERYWHERE YOU LOOK in nature, members of one species hang with members of their own kind. You see it in the barnyard: sheep with sheep, ducks with ducks, cows with cows — in the woods: squirrels with squirrels, bunnies with bunnies, deer with deer — under the ground: ants with ants — in the water: dolphins with dolphins.

But I also see that within a flock like-breed will congregate with like-breed. It is quite obvious that a Buff Orpington's best friends are the other Buffs. If the birds don't have a same-breed companion the most similar partner up. Blue, our white and black rooster, roosts at night beside the hen most similar to him — a White Rock. I don't see this as a shunning or exclusive practice. It is still a single flock, and, as alpha rooster, Blue defends every hen with equal ferociousness.

As a species, humans are not much different from chickens in terms of hanging with the one most like you are. But our alliances quickly go into territory unfamiliar to the so-called dumber beasts. Discrimination is not a part of God's created design and is surely a sorrow to Him.

We would do better not to take our status of children of God as overly special. We are a part of his creation. Scripture says that all of creation will be reconciled to Him. I understand this to include not just the people, his children, but all of creation: his chickens, his trees, his rivers. St. Paul writes in Romans (8:21) that the whole creation has been groaning in labor pains. Whether we are experiencing the pains of birth or the agony of death I cannot say but the moans of earth are growing louder by the day.

The prophet Isaiah talks about the Kingdom of God where the

wolf lays down with the lamb. It is hard to imagine a time or place in which we don't divide the world into categories of predator or prey, friend or foe. He describes a new balance that is foreign to our daily experience. I catch a glimpse of this vision at dusk when the wild bunnies of the wood come and graze with my chickens. Feeding side by side, the one is not scared of or intimidated by the other. A hush and peace descends upon the land. There is a sense that rest awaits, rest for all of creation, in the ever-loving arms of our Maker who made us all.

Blues for Blue

BLUE LASTED ONE WEEK after being overthrown from his Alpha status. I'm not sure he saw it coming. Maybe he did. I didn't. Is there not a place for a grandfather in the community of chickens? Denied entrance to the coop, injured, wet and cold after days of exposure to rain, he ended up as a pile of feathers here and a pile of feathers there on the morning of the seventh day.

The Sunday before, it was all fight and confrontation from the Blue Andalusia we call B-Rock. Hackles out, a show-down of charge, counter-charge, and ninja summersaults, I could see it would be a long and bad day for Blue if I kept the birds penned so I opened the gate early. Even so, Blue lost the fight. Bloodied and pitiful he stayed well out of harm's way the rest of the day trying to regain his strength and dignity. That night B-Rock denied him entrance not only to the coop but to the interior of the pen as well. Blue wailed miserably as he retreated to seek other safe haven.

He ended up in the unused dog house. In the middle of the night I heard him squawk, and rising to look out the window, saw him tear out across the lawn, white feathers visible in the light of the full moon. He woke up Monday, having lived through two near-death experiences within the 24-hour period. In the process he had lost one of his wickedly long spurs, his best asset, a critical loss.

Blue picked some more fights with B-Rock trying to regain his crown but it was not to be. Blue was an ancient three years old, B-Rock an uppity one-year old. Blue was smaller in stature and lighter in weight. And Blue was hurt more. I would see Blue give a charge and think "Don't do it. Accept the number two position." But that wasn't part of his nature.

Maybe it isn't part of our nature either. Who wants to get older, lose status, and lose control? Who wants to be second in the affections of the family circle? Who wants to be the one that stands out in the rain? We try to extend our Alpha looks as long as we can: dye our hair, work out, get nips and tucks. Maybe we're afraid there isn't a place for the grandfather, for the grandmother in our world. And, maybe there isn't.

I have heard that Canadian geese, when flying on their great migrations, take care of their injured and infirm. If one falls behind because of sickness or injury one goose will partner up with the injured, land, and stay with him until he has recovered, or dies, and then resume their or his flight. I prefer that example in nature.

God doesn't stop caring just because we get older. Jesus showed mercy and tenderness to those who had become, for whatever reason, marginalized; those who were no longer or would never be the Alpha of their community. We're all going down at some point. Better to show mercy, have pity, and be empathetic. It's a dance: as one slows down, one speeds up; one lets go, one picks up; one receives, one gives.

I believe B-Rock could have benefited from Blue's continued presence in the flock. There's a lot of territory to cover, a lot of sky to watch, a lot of ladies to handle. He didn't think Blue could be a grandfather. Blue didn't know how to be one.

We, however, should know better but somehow miss it too. For thousands of years people have had to be reminded by the prophets to take care of the widow and the orphan. It must not come naturally. Survival of the fittest is the deeper part of our nature but not the better part. The 5th commandment, as my mother likes to remind me, is the only one that comes with a blessing: "Honor your father and your mother, so that your days may be long in the land that the Lord your God is giving you." (Exodus 20:26)

Honor must be taught. Honor is a discipline. What we have been told to do becomes our responsibility to do. We know better because we have heard it from God, our maker. I don't know if God's commandments are written on the hearts of chickens. I don't know if He told them or not. I can tell the chickens to honor their elders but they don't seem to be inclined to listen to me.

So I've got the blues for Blue:

I got the blues for Blue, I feel so bad for you
I miss you doodledoo, I'm crying tears boohoo

Thanksgiving

OUR NIECE, BETHANY and her husband, Steve, were driving down from Harrisonburg, Virginia, with a nice sized pumpkin in the car — a pumpkin from the Shenandoah Valley. Deeply orange, it matched the autumn-tinged leaves in the third week of November. Thanksgiving: the gathering of the tribe.

We weren't sure whether the pumpkin would end up being eaten as pie or bread or whether it would have an ornamental use. Mom decided to use the pumpkin as an outside decoration and put it in the tended area beside the back door. It was a logical spot and looked cheerful under the bird feeder.

Our chickens are regular visitors to the area under their bird feeder picking up the tidbits left behind from cardinals, finch, nuthatch, and sparrows. In fact, our chickens are as at home in their yard as in ours. They tend not to notice or recognize property lines. They like to head over there at first light especially in the fall and winter when the mornings are cool. The folks keep water pistols handy when the chickens start scratching near plants they would rather not be disturbed. They say chickens can be trained using water as a deterrent and maybe that is so. The intelligence of chickens should not be underestimated.

Chickens are not fussy eaters — they eat most everything: grain, bugs, fruits, and vegetables (not so crazy about cabbage though). They love ripe plums, crusts of bread, corncobs, steak trimmings, cantaloupe rinds, and especially sunflower seeds. They are not very discriminating, to the point of being, ugh, cannibalistic. I have found them eating a fallen sister whose remains a hawk left behind. They will approach an unknown food source with an equal amount of curiosity and suspicion. The rooster usually weighs in with an opinion, and finally, a brave hen will take a peck and then they all fall into the attack.

Of course the sheer size of the pumpkin made eating it daunting. But the chickens applied themselves to the task at hand. Little did we know at the outset that consuming the pumpkin would not be the primary focus, the carving of the pumpkin was the higher calling.

By the end of the first day, the whole thing had a feathered look. Small pecks over the entire surface gave the pumpkin a textured and, yes, feathered appearance. A potter using a knife on the still-soft clay could not have done a more thorough and even job.

On day two the sculpting work began. The pumpkin was by now on its side with the stem parallel to the ground. As the chickens started eating the pumpkin a shape began to emerge. A shape that looked very much like . . . a chicken shape! The stem was the beak, a raised area in the back was a tail, and raised areas on the sides suggested wings.

The chickens seemed satisfied with their work and left it alone after that. They had created a monument celebrating the year of the chicken; it was the zenith of their development. I am so glad I was able to witness this historic achievement and record it for all posterity.

LET IT BE KNOWN THAT ON THANKSGIVING DAY, NOVEMBER 23, 2007,
OUR CHICKENS FASHIONED A LIKENESS OF THEIR OWN KIND
WITH LITTLE FANFARE OR FUSS

Or, maybe it was an offering of thankfulness straight from their communal heart. I know chickens can be happy. They make happy sounds, contented sounds. I know chickens live with hope. This is expressed when they run to our side looking for special treats. All creation knows how to return thanks to the Creator. Birds sing, fall trees shimmer with radiant color, brooks and streams ripple and laugh — all without prompting. We humans are the only ones that need to be reminded to do so. It has required a national holiday for goodness sake.

Tom and I are thankful for the time of shared table with those who mean the most to us, the promise of health restored to our niece Katie, evenings of song and board games, afternoons of walking through the woods, and visits with our neighbors and their farm animals.

After Thanksgiving the family disperses again. Our northern branch returns to Chicago, the college-aged cousins return to their respective schools. Bethany and Steve drive back to Virginia. Tom and I, Mom and Dad remain — as do the chickens.

God is good and loves a thankful heart.

I'm pretty sure He appreciated the chickens' pumpkin sculpture.

The chicken's Thanksgiving sculpture with one of the hens giving it a final inspection.

Winter Wonderland

A HEN'S EGG PRODUCTION is very much based on the amount of light in the day. We had just passed the Winter Solstice when the days begin to lengthen and nights begin to shorten. I was astonished that the number of eggs laid began to increase slowly but steadily starting December 21. December 21 is also heading straight into the North Carolina winter, mild though it may be. We get snow from time to time in North Carolina. It's always an occasion.

I love the way the snow looks when it's coming down and the air of stillness when it no longer falls. I love the way it absorbs sound creating a holy peace. I love the flash of the cardinal's red against the white of the snow; the way the wild birds quickly find the seed we put out for them; the way life slows down and you are not expected to be at work on time because it's a snow storm.

Chickens don't like snow.

They don't like to look at it and they don't like to walk out in it. In fact, they would rather go hungry and thirsty than venture out of their coop over the snow to their provisions. Unless I go out and make a path of straw from the coop to the food they are resolved to wait until it goes away. A rainstorm they endure with stoicism. A cold white surfaced ground cover is cause for dismay and retreat.

Other critters don't like the snow either. Mr. Possum didn't like the snow. Mr. Possum thought he had found a nice warm snuggly place to sleep and wait it out.

I thought something was up when five birds did not return to roost inside the chicken house come nightfall. They ranged from the most timed (White Orpington) to the most courageous (Dark Cornish). Of course, I immediately considered a lurking predator. So with flashlight in hand and a sense of suspicion I went to investigate. The perimeter seemed unbroken, the coop seemed full of more trusting chickens and so I said "It's OK you can go to bed" and they followed the light inside. I closed up the house, for warmth, and I closed up the pen for protection.

The next morning I went to let them out and in the top front nesting box was a little pointy face with the coloration of our Light Brahmas and I said "Whoa Nelly you are not a chicken." And Mr. Possum said "I'm a chicken. I'm a chicken." But he did the sensible thing and left.

There were no eggs that afternoon. I figured Mr. Possum had helped himself but I didn't see him around anywhere. Chickens went into the house fine that night.

The next morning, I let them out and there again in the top front nesting box was the same little pointy face with the coloration of our Light Brahmas and I said "WHOA Nelly you are NOT a chicken." And Mr. Possum said "I AM a chicken. I AM a chicken."

I called in the tactical support of my husband and he dispatched, on a permanent basis, Mr. Possum.

However, after living through two whole days of mortal danger the hens refused to lay eggs. They did not lay eggs for three weeks. Or rather, over the course of three weeks the total number of eggs I collected from 34 laying hens was five. Can't say I can blame them. Chickens have been known to drop dead from fright. Our neighbors lost 110 chickens one night — some killed by a dog — but most killed by their own panic.

Maybe Mr. Possum really did think he was a chicken. Maybe with a day's worth of eggs in his belly, he was stuffed, contented, and sleepy. I'm surprised we lost no birds during this episode. We were lucky. But it did not seem wise to depend on this. The prospects for a good long-term relationship were not high.

The weeks passed, the days continued to get longer, the snow melted, warmer temperatures prevailed, and gradually the hens returned to their egg production. All is well in the backyard again.

Christmas Eve in the Barn

THERE IS A FOLKLORE STORY that on Christmas Eve at midnight animals are given the gift of speech for one hour. This is said to be an expression of God's gratitude for the comforting presence of the animals in the stable during the birth of the baby Jesus. I was not aware of this story during my childhood growing up outside of Philadelphia; it has only been in the years of living in the country that I have been introduced to this traditional tale. Our neighbors across the road, to honor the animals during their time of being honored by God, invite friends and neighbors over to their barn to sing carols to their animals on Christmas Eve.

This has become somewhat of a pilgrimage for us. We bundle up and trudge across the road to join others in song. We sing our favorites: *Joy to the World, Silent Night,* and *The First Noel* (the ones you mostly know the words of) to the cows, goats, sheep, and angora rabbits. The barn has been beautified with twinkle lights and a large lit star. Joy and Bob provide hay for us to feed the (for the most part mute and disinterested) cattle. After a while, we are sung out and cold and go our separate ways after heartily wishing everyone Merry Christmas.

I can imagine the comforting presence of animals in the stable long ago. I can see the heat rising from their bodies and their eyes taking in the scene. They would have waited with Joseph as Mary labored through the night.

I don't imagine the presence of chickens. They would have been as totally oblivious that night as on any other. Chickens go into a trance-like state when darkness comes. An hour before sunset, they begin their trek home to their roost. They chow down one last time, get a long drink of water, and go find their spot in the coop. Once it is dark, you can move among them with impunity, pick up even a rooster without a qualm. They are in another zone.

So while we may wonder about the truth of the Christmas legend, we suspend logic and come to the barn ready for a miracle on Christmas Eve. Will they speak to us this year? Maybe it will be the sheep, perhaps the calf — definitely not the chicken. I'm pretty sure God would have excluded them from the gift of speech since it's highly likely they slept through the events of the first Christmas when Jesus was birthed in the stable.

The ONLY basis I can imagine that they might be given the gift of speech is if the rooster's first crow of Christmas morn heralded the news of the birth. If that was the case, I think chickens would be deserving of a miracle, so I will listen for the chicken voice amongst the stable animals after all.

O, Freedom

Now the Lord is the spirit, and where the Spirit of the Lord is, there is freedom. — (II Corinthians 3:17)

MY DEAR FRIEND, Lise Uyanik, and I have been singing the spiritual *O, Freedom* for 30-some years. Whenever we sing it, a hush falls and people listen with an air of reverence.

Everyone knows what freedom is and longs for it. *"Lord for me, Lord for me,"* the words repeat. We yearn for freedom from that which binds us, hurts us, and weighs us down. *"No more weeping, no more moaning,"* the song implores. We choose freedom no matter the cost. *"And before I be a slave, I be buried in my grave."*

In the song, *Count My Heart,* by fellow songwriter Kathleen

Hannan, about the first democratic elections in South Africa, which were held in 1944, the chorus proclaims:

Freedom is coming
Freedom is coming
Freedom is coming, we paid with our lives
Because no one gives freedom away

In our fallen world, freedom is not free. Societies and people work and fight to achieve political, economic, intellectual, and religious freedom denied to them by those in power. Dogs strain against the leash; tigers pace within the cage; apes rattle their bars; water finds its way around the dam. It seems as if all of creation recognizes the difference between freedom and confinement.

On a more benign level, we grapple with the tension between freedom and responsibility, safety, order, and the comfort of routine. After our experience with the dreaded hawk, Tom increased the chickens' run space and enclosed the penned area fully, top and sides. For us, to continue to keep the chickens free meant certain death, whereas imprisonment offered life. We temper their captivity with the opportunity to roam when we come home from work and on the weekends, but they are now mostly confined.

In the afternoons they listen for the car's arrival. The rooster is always positioned to see around the corner of the house. When he sees one of us, he crows to let the ladies know: release is at hand. All the birds get excited and rush toward the door of the pen, trying to be first out.

They return at dusk on their own, or at least most do. We have a Black Australorpe who has decided she'll take freedom at any cost. Sleeping in a tree — unprotected during the summer is one thing, during the winter it is quite another. She has no nest or leaves to deflect the wind. When it is cold she has no companion to snuggle against; when it is rainy she gets wet. She has no protection from owl and raccoon on the prowl at night or from dog and hawk during the day. She has no access to our provisions of water and feed and must be responsible for finding her own source of nourishment. She will, I fear, not live as long as her sister hens, but it will be on her own terms.

We rationalize the new arrangement for the birds with the thought, "It's for their own good." But it is also in our self-interest: we want the eggs. Unfortunately, the eggs are not quite as good; the yolks don't have that high marigold-yellow color. We are denying freedom to the birds; our Black Australorpe is gambling with her life. Nobody is winning. Even the hawk is working harder these days.

St. Paul, writing from captivity, knows where true freedom is to be found: "Where the spirit of the Lord is, there is freedom." Again, I find myself thinking that when God reconciles the world to Himself, all creation will find perfect freedom. The "freedoms from" will be no more; the "freedoms to" will be ever present. We will not have to fight for the freedom that God promises. It is His gift.

O Freedom concludes with this same powerful sentiment and declaration: My home is with God. And in His kingdom is true freedom.

O Freedom, O Freedom, O Freedom
Lord for me, Lord for me.
And before I be a slave, I be buried in my grave
And go home to my Lord and be free.

Addendum.
So many eggs, so little time

RECIPES

Apple Pancake

After working for so many years in the food industry, having my own restaurant and then working with Whole Foods Market I pretty much have lost any interest in cooking. I do however still enjoy baking and making breakfasts for special mornings. Here's a great recipe I have adapted from Anna Thomas' *The Vegetarian Epicure,* a favorite cookbook of mine. (serves 4–6). I always make this on Christmas and Easter mornings.

- Peel and slice up 4 apples and sauté them in 2 T butter with ¼ cup brown sugar and cinnamon (to taste) until soft and somewhat caramelized — set aside
- Whisk together 3 eggs with ¾ cup of unbleached flour then add ¾ cup milk and ¼ t salt. (It should be a very smooth batter.)
- Melt 2 T butter in a large iron fry pan — add batter
- Put the fry pan (and batter) in a 450° oven for 10 minutes. Be prepared to prick it with a fork when it rises in a bubble formation
- Turn down the oven to 350° and continue baking until done (around 15 minutes)
- Turn pancake out on a serving plate and spread with softened cream cheese; add the cooked apples
- Fold it in half like you would an omelet, sprinkle it with powdered sugar, and serve immediately with maple syrup and bacon.

Quiche

Just so you know, I am very bad about measuring.

My crusts are made with 1 stick of butter, 1 very full cup of unbleached flour, and a little salt.

I let the butter sit out until it is soft, then add the flour and salt and hand mix until it is crumbly, evenly textured, feels damp, and will hold holder together when you put a clump in your hand and squeeze. Then I add a small amount of cold water until it begins to come together and can hold itself as a ball.

For the innards I use 4 eggs, 1 ½ cup of milk or half and half, and a least 2 cups of grated Swiss cheese (I don't measure — it should look generous in the pie pan). Bake at 350° for about 45 minutes or until it puffs up, gets golden-brown highlights, and no longer jiggles.

For combinations of ingredients I like:

- Artichoke hearts, roasted red pepper, green onions, & feta cheese
- Ham & fresh spinach
- Bacon & caramelized onions
- Salmon, green onion & capers
- Sausage & sautéed sweet peppers

I do not like chicken in quiche — somehow that just seems wrong.

Pound Cake

This is a great way to use up eggs, especially in the spring with the hens are laying a lot and there are fresh strawberries and raspberries around.

- Cream ½# of butter with 1 ⅔ cup of sugar until light and fluffy.
- Add 5 eggs, one at a time, beating thoroughly between eggs.
- Add 1 teaspoon of vanilla
- Add and mix by hand 2 cups of pre-sifted unbleached flour to which ½ t salt and ½ t baking powder have been added. Beat until smooth.
- Spoon into a buttered and floured bread pan.
- Put in a 325° oven and bake until done — at least an hour.
- Let sit a few minutes before turning out of the pan.

Fried Potatoes & Eggs

This is my favorite breakfast, lunch, or dinner when I am eating by myself and have a left-over baked potato in the refrigerator. I would rather save a baked potato for another day than eat one hot and flaky at dinner.

- Sauté some onion until caramelized in a cast iron fry pan
- Add cut up left-over potato and cook until nicely browned
- Add any number of other things often other left-overs (sweet peppers, eggplant, or squash)
- Add some kind of pig product: bacon, pepperoni slices, Genoa salami, left over roast pork or ham
- Finally add one or two eggs and when cooked it's as you like it add grated cheese, salt, and fresh ground black pepper
- YUMmmmmmm

Aunt Clara's Apple Cake

My father's Aunt Clara was a fabulous baker and I make this cake often for the fall market.

* Peel and slice up 4 apples, set aside
* Cream 4 eggs with 1 cup oil (I use canola) and 2 cups of sugar
* Mix with 3 cups unbleached flour and 1 T baking powder
* Add: 2 ½ teaspoon vanilla and ⅓ cup orange juice
* Spoon ½ of the batter into a greased bundt pan
* Arrange ½ of the apples over the batter and sprinkle with cinnamon sugar
* Spoon 2nd half of batter on top and arrange the 2nd half of the apples on top and sprinkle with cinnamon sugar

Bake at 350°.
It takes forever, way more than one hour.

Pecan Pie

My father loves this pie, so I dedicate it to him.

Use the quiche piecrust recipe but add a little sugar.

Toast 2 cups pecans in the oven (350° 5–8 minutes) to bring out their flavor then put them in the pie pan.

Whisk together the following ingredients, then pour over the pecans:

* 3 eggs
* ¾ cup sugar
* ¾ cup light corn syrup
* ⅛ teaspoon salt
* 1 teaspoon vanilla

Bake at 425° for 10 minutes, reduce heat to 350° and continue to bake until done around 35 minutes.

www.ingramcontent.com/pod-product-compliance
Ingram Content Group UK Ltd.
Pitfield, Milton Keynes, MK11 3LW, UK
UKHW041916190726
13854UKWH00003B/1267

9 780557 746736